THE NEED FOR HAWAI'I

A GUIDE TO HAWAIIAN CULTURAL and KAHUNA VALUES

by

Patrick Ka'ano'i

Published by:

KA'ANO'I PRODUCTIONS
P.O. Box 104976 • Jefferson City, MO 65110

First Edition 1991
Second Edition 1992

Copyright 1992 Patrick Ka'ano'i

All rights reserved. No part of this booklet may be reproduced or transmitted in any form or by any means, electronic or mechanical, including photocopying, recording or by any information storage or retrieval system without written permission from the author, except for the inclusion of brief quotations in a review.

ISBN 0-9623654-3-2

Allow yourself to know, for with knowledge comes confidence and from confidence comes harmony.

ACKNOWLEDGEMENTS

It is with sincere appreciation and aloha that I recognize Heinke Leialoha, my wife, for her unceasing support, and love, to the members of the Kū Kanaka sub-committee on Hawaiian religious values for recognizing The Need For Hawai'i, to Carol Cornicelli, Florence Kelley and her sister who edited this booklet.

To you Jeff Munoz, Doya Nardin and Don Triaka Smith thank you for listening with your hearts and minds.

And special thoughts for the late Napua Stevens for her support, and the late Lokomaika'i Snakenberg who helped introduce to our mo'opuna the true value of all things Hawaiian.

I give to you all my love and aloha.

ABOUT THE AUTHOR

Patrick Ka'ano'i is a native of Hawai'i of Hawaiian and Portuguese ancestry and founder of a Hawaiian Philosophical organization called The Huna Hanauna Society. He is a full time entertainer and composer with more than 40 educational television programs to his credit. He is also founder of *Lā Hae Hawai'i-Hawaiian Flag Day* in Hawai'i as well as co-author of *The Hawaiian Name Book* and author of various published articles on Hawaiian values.

CONTENTS

INTRODUCTION 1

CHAPTER ONE - What are Hawaiian Kahuna Values? . . 5
* Is There a Hawaiian Church? 5
* Subjective to Objective 6
* Family Worship 7
* The God 8
* No Satan 8
* Science 8
* Philosophy and Religion 9

CHAPTER TWO - 'Ohana - Family 11
* Makua - Parent 11
* Ho'okipa - Hospitality 11
* At a Lu'au or Party 12
* Kupuna - Grandparent 12
* 'Aumakua - Spirit Ancestor 12
* Akua - Distant Spirit Ancestor 13
* Ali'i - Parent of the People 13
* Ho'oponopono - Setting Right 14
* Pō - The After Life 16
* There Is No Hell 17

CHAPTER THREE - Aloha - Love 19
* The Living Expression of Aloha 19
* Dualism of Love 20
* The Purpose of Aloha 20
* Everlasting Love 21
* Aloha 'Oe - May You BeLoved 21

CONTENTS

CHAPTER FOUR - Pa'ahana - Industry · · · · · · · 23
* The Family · · · · · · · · · · · · 23
* Mana - Power and Work Ethics · · · · · · 23
* Hawaiian and Western Work Ethics · · · · 23
* Apply the Hawaiian Work Ethic · · · · · · 24
* The Work Place · · · · · · · · · · · 25
* Management · · · · · · · · · · · · 25
* Your Own Company · · · · · · · · · · 25

CHAPTER FIVE - Maika'i - Excellence · · · · · · 27
* Male Symbol of Excellence · · · · · · · 27
* Personal Mana - Power · · · · · · · · 27
* Increase Your Excellence · · · · · · · · 28
* Prayer - Pule · · · · · · · · · · · · 28

SUGGESTED READING · · · · · · · · · · · 29

INTRODUCTION

Is there a need for Hawai'i? In recent years a new understanding of the environment, and our relationship to nature has introduced a concept fundamental to subjective oriented cultures: That man should *empower* or *ho'omanamana* instead of overpower nature. To concede that man is a part of nature and therefore affected by nature is the fundamental truth and hope of our future. Although new to the West, this subjective oriented concept is fundamental to the Hawaiian culture. The experience of the Hawaiian culture, in its relationship to man and nature, stands out as a resource and beacon of hope for all who would value **The Need for Hawai'i**.

It is said that to understand a culture's values is to understand that culture's philosophy. In recent years there has been an unfolding of literature on Hawaiian values and the need to understand and apply them. **The Need For Hawai'i** is a contribution to these works from another perspective, that of a non-Christian religious and philosophical approach, hereafter referred to as *Hawaiian Kahuna Values*.

Hawaiian religious philosophy is the foundation of Hawaiian values. However, Hawaiian religious philosophy or *Kahunaism* has been one of the most misunderstood aspect of Hawaiian culture.

With the introduction of Christian missions to Hawai'i in 1820, any hope of the study and comprehension of Hawaiian thought simply came to an end. A new era of anti-Hawaiian thought took hold and permeated every aspect of Hawaiian society and government. Ironically, the missionaries thankfully committed the spoken Hawaiian into a written language. Thanks to some Hawaiian and non-Hawaiian scholars, some valuable records of Hawaiian culture have come down to us in writing.

Today all thoughtful hearts and minds know that this early Christian approach to Hawaiian culture was wrong and have since made some major contributions to setting it right.

The public and private school systems have now introduced Hawaiian studies, values and language to their curriculum. Hawaiians are now seeking solidarity and self determination to introduce their value systems into law. In 1967 the Hawai'i State Legislature amended a law to allow the giving of non-Christian first names to children born in Hawai'i. Before 1967 it was illegal to have a Hawaiian first name. In 1978 the United States Congress passed the Native American Freedom of Religion Act giving Hawaiians, as well as Native Americans, religious freedom.

The formal introduction for a forum of Hawaiian thought came about in 1985 by a native Hawaiian philosophical society called The Huna Hanauna Society. This organization formally opened the door for the contemporary study and application of Hawaiian religious philosophy or **Kahunaism**.. A four year study by this organization revealed there is a desire to understand and apply native Hawaiian spiritual and philosophical values for our time.

What can you do now? The first step is to open your mind and seek out the knowledge and experience of Kahuna values. Read this book and others like it. Whether you are Hawaiian or not, if you believe in Hawai'i, then say so. If you are a Christian or of another faith, allow yourself to know, for with knowledge comes confidence, and from confidence comes harmony.

The purpose of this book is to identify, understand and Hawaiian religious philosophy and specific Hawaiian K Values for our time. The cornerstones of Hawaiian K na Values are: *'Ohana*-Family, *Aloha*-Love, *Pa'ahana*-Industry and *Maika'i*-Excellence. These values will help you understand and succeed in areas regarding:

- A. Family
- B. Health
- C. Education
- D. Nature
- E. Business
- F. Government

There will always be a land, a people, a language, and a culture called Hawai'i. The personal values and nature of Hawai'i as a peaceful nation are a cultural resource and contribution to world society. We have felt her heart; now let us hear her voice.

Grammatical Markers

Please note that a *macron* (−) placed above a vowel has a long sound. The glottal stop or *okina* (') has a short sound as in "Oh-Oh".

4 NOTES

CHAPTER ONE

WHAT ARE HAWAIIAN KAHUNA VALUES?

Hawaiian Kahuna Values are Hawaiian religious and philosophical values for our time. Traditionally spiritual and philosophical knowledge is held by the *kahuna* or specialists. Since 1820 much of the kahuna knowledge has been fragmented and consequently is very difficult to understand. This work is offered as a general guide to the fundamental principles of kahuna values and their application to everyday life and beyond.

Is There A Hawaiian Church?
There is no Hawaiian church comparable to Western religion. Worship is generally practiced at home with a family altar or *kuahu*. This altar may be composed of any *meaningful* symbols or pictures of family or things. The intent of the symbols presented on this altar is to empower ones life with inspiration and hope to succeed in and celebrate life. A formal temple or *heiau*, when in perfect condition and dedicated without flaw, is generally for chiefs or *ali'i*.

Farmers and fishermen also may have an altar. A farmer may use a specially chosen upright stone in the corner of his field or taro patch. The fisherman might create a *ko'a*, which consists of an upright stone at the seashore elevated and surrounded at the base by coral pebbles. Both upright stones are to be empowered with meaning to inspire one's skills for success.

Subjective to Objective

All cultures and individuals are both subjective and objective. However, depending on our individual or cultural backgrounds, we may be primarily more subjective or objective in our relationship to one another and society. Identifying our subjective or objective nature and things in our lives is the first step to empowering a better life. From the following list, identify what you think is subjective and objective.

      Yourself   Money   Family   Government
      Computers Car   Schools Technology
      Creativity Religion Love   Philosophy

How can you tell? Simply ask yourself which is human or personal, and which is not. What is human is subjective and what is not is objective. Yourself, family, love, religion, philosophy, and creativity are all subjective. Money, car, computers, technology, schools, and government institutions are objective. Any item you identified incorrectly probably indicates a possible area of frustration and misunderstanding. You don't have to be confused if you understand.

Like individuals, cultures are also primarily subjective or objective. The culture that primarily values technology or individualism is definitely objective, while a culture that values the family, nature, and the celebration of life is surely identified as subjective. Whether you are Hawaiian or not, if you primarily relate to life and people on a personal level, you are subjective and have a major conflict of interest in the present Western objective style of ethics. What can you do about it?

The secret of a subjective individual or culture within an objective one is simply to *draw a circle bigger than the one that shuts you out*. Don't be afraid of objective tools or systems, for it is the subjective self that empowers them, not the other way around. Government, money, and technology are not human, and don't make the mistake of thinking they are. Use them creatively, and you will command your life, family, and culture.

If you have identified yourself as more objective than subjective in nature, the preceding information will be your resource for understanding your subjective or personal nature and that of those around you.

Family Worship
Early Christian missionaries who came to Hawai'i generally, through their self-imposed ignorance, considered Hawaiians as pagan, unenlightened, demonic nature worshipers. The truth of the matter is that the Hawaiian culture is founded on the love of family. How, then, could loving one's family be remotely misconstrued as pagan or unenlightened?

The family is the entire society of Hawaiian people, personal and subjective. From the *keiki*-child to *makua*-parent, and *kupuna*- grandparent, from *ali'i*-parent chief of the culture to beyond the human realm of the spirit, to *'aumakua*-deceased ancestor and *akua*-distant spirit ancestor. All are in the realm of the *'ohana*, family.

The God

The Hawaiian translation of the Bible uses the word *akua* to mean **The God.** However, no scholar can find such a true Hawaiian word for The God concept in Christian dogma. The closest equivalent to the Christian God concept is regarded as what is self-evident and obvious, or nature itself. The Hawaiian interpretation of *akua* is the best and most beloved of one's distant ancestors and of human origin.

No Satan

Since Hawaiian thought is based on excellence and the value of being beloved, we have to take responsibility for all our actions.

Consequently, we do not blame or assign a flaw or error in our judgment or action to an invisible being. The concept of Satan does not exist in the Hawaiian culture. We are personally responsible and accountable for our own actions and deeds.

Science

It has been observed that Hawaiians never developed a high level of objective science or technology. However the inspiration of science is wonder, and the reward is discovery. The Hawaiians voyage across the ocean and the development of their culture are direct results of their unquenchable capacity for wonder and discovery, their greatness being no less than the feats equivalent to flying modern man into the cosmos and colonizing the stars.

These voyaging accomplishments are a direct result of what I call a *subjective science*. This form of science maximized the human potential with a minimum of technology. Imagine such a science empowering the objective sciences of today. The possibility opens a new frontier of discovery and understanding.

Philosophy and Religion

Kahuna values identify philosophy and religion as two natural components of creative thought. Philosophy is defined here as a system of living life, while religion is the hope of what is not known. It's curious that critical thinkers of the West usually discredit the value of religious thought while retaining the value of philosophy; and yet religious philosophy is comparable to scientific and theoretical processes. Consider the origin of the cosmos or the creation of man. Both science and religion have a system of explanation that seems to work, and both have a hope that they are correct. Scientific theory and religious hope are one and the same in Hawaiian Kahuna Values. The only difference between religious and scientific theory is that science is more contemporary and updated while religion has the tendency to be outdated and closed minded. Religion doesn't have to be closed minded or outdated. Transcend this misunderstanding and feel free to explore your human potential of mind and spirit, and life will unfold as a blossom. Let your life bloom in your heart and mind.

10 NOTES

'OHANA - FAMILY

The foundation of Hawaiian culture is the family, and spiritual relationship of the family commands the very essence of human values found in every part of everyday life. It is in the family that we identify the individual, the family unit, community, government and spiritual ideals.

The values applied here are *aloha*-love, *ho'okipa*-hospitality, *pa'ahana*-industry, *ho'oponopono*-setting right, and *lōkāhi* -unity.

Makua-The Parent

The symbol of the parent is the symbol of the duality of life. Parents are both male and female, *kāne* and *wahine*. From their union of *aloha* comes the child. Children are the blossoms of marriage. When a man and a woman live and love together, they are married, and their responsibility of man and wife begins there. Marriage doesn't always require a formal document or ceremony.

The responsibility of the parent is to establish a home and set an example of love, unity and industry.

Ho'okipa-Hospitality

It is the parents' responsibility to show an example of hospitality to all who would come to their home. Comfort, food and companionship are shared with all guests, who are greeted with *aloha* and the touching of nose to cheek. Children are introduced by the parent but are not to be overly talkative. While adults are left to one another's company, children of the household are obliged to show the same hospitality with their youthful guest, away from the adults.

At a Luau or Party
How often have you attended a *lu'au*-party and not know what was going on, except for having an invitation and knowing just a face or two. This is not the Hawaiian way. At a *luau* guests should always be greeted and attended by the host or hostess or appointed family member. Children of adolescent age are appropriate hosts and hostesses for the family. The greeters should be mannerly in expressing their aloha sincerely and be knowledgeable of their family and event.

The *malihini*-guest is always thoughtful to express his/her appreciation, not to overstay the hosts' hospitality, and always to bear some gift of appreciation to that household.

Kupuna-The Grandparent
The *kupuna*-grandparent is a resource of wisdom, love and *mana*-divine power or authority. It is the grandparent who gives the inspired name to a *mo'opuna*-grandchild of *koko*-blood or *hānai*-adoption. The grandparent passes on his/her gifts of acquired talents and *mana* within their life time to designated grandchildren.

'Aumakua-The Spirit Ancestor
An *'aumakua* is a personal spirit ancestor. Contrary to some popular belief, an *'aumakua* is not an earthbound or transfigured

body of one's ancestor, such as a lizard, owl, or shark. These symbols are the *kino lau*-body symbol of ones spirit ancestor. The *kino lau* of ones *'aumakua* is an empowered memory or sign of one's departed ancestor. The real spirit of one's ancestor resides in *pō*-the spirit realm.

Akua-The Distant Spirit Ancestor
The *akua* represents the best of one's distant spirit ancestors. The memory of their greatness is represented by the value of being most loved. No greater value is placed in this life or the next than in being beloved by our family. And so it is with our *akua* and their *kino lau* arching as the rainbow, full moon, sun or stars that shine in the sky.

Aliʻi-The Parent of the People
Before there were **aliʻi**-chiefs, there was the parent. Later when the family grew into a complex community, the need for a community representative became apparent. This representative or parent of the community, chosen for his excellence, is called the *aliʻi,* the one who *shines supreme*. His purpose was to manage and identify his family community and his reward was their love, their *aloha.*

In contrast to Western style government, the form of government with an *aliʻi* at its head was subjective first and objective second. The success of a chosen *aliʻi* member of Hawaiian society was contingent on his ability in having his people or family succeed in and celebrate life. The system of government and *kapu*-sanctity or taboo managed by the *aliʻi* was merely an objective system empowered subjectively and personally by the people and their love.

Ho'oponopono-Setting Right
The harmony of any family is accomplished by communicating with the heart and mind. As in all human relationships, emotions and situations arise that test one's ability to relate to one another and cope with everyday life. A system of setting things right is called *ho'oponopono*.

Communication is the key to the success of *ho'oponopono*. A session of *ho'oponopono* is practiced at least once a year. There is no need to wait till a major misunderstanding or difficulty to arise.

The process of *ho'oponopono* requires that all members of the family agree to an *'uao*-mediator. This mediator could be a respected male or female adult who is empowered by the family to be the final word in the family discussion and healing process. The role of the mediator is to allow the process of everyone's communication of heart and mind to unfold. The mediator is not to make or offer judgment, only to allow the healing process of nature to take effect.

The outpouring of emotion is common in *ho'oponopono*. Tears, laughter, hugging, and kissing are all part of the unspoken process of healing and bonding of family members. Following is a general guide to the process. You may create your own setting or traditions agreed to by everyone involved.

1. Identify an *'uao*-mediator.
   A. Male or female member of family or community.
   B. Mature and unbiased.
   C. Familiar or trained in *ho'oponopono*.
2. Identify the family situation.
   A. Set a date.
   B. Ascertain the situation to be resolved.
   C. Determine the members concerned.
   D. Invite appropriate family members to attend.
3. Open meeting by mediator.
   A. Mediator asks members of the family if they agree to his or her mediation and also explains the purpose of their meeting.
   B. Mediator explains his or her role.
   C. The mediator may open with a ***pule***-prayer.
      1) This *pule* is composed to ask ones *'aumakua*-spirit ancestor by name or the memory of that *'aumakua* to inspire them for success with love and *aloha*. This *pule* may be in Hawaiian or English.
4. *Ho'oponopono* begins.
   A. The mediator asks members concerned to freely express their side of the story one at a time.
   B. The mediator allows time for emotional outpouring.
   C. The mediator asks members concerned to allow forgiveness to be a part of the healing process.
   D. The process closes with touching and the expressing of *aloha*.
   E. The family mediator ends by asking the family if his service was ***maika'i***-excellent . If it

is, then the response is *ae*-yes. The mediator then closes with a prayer and ends with the words **'āmama**-it is finished, **ua noa**-it is free. After the prayer a closing statement appropriate to the family tradition, may be used.
   F. If possible, the *ho'oponopono* ceremony should continue with an unlimited time and commitment of family members. A sincere *ho'oponopono* ceremony should continue until it is pronounced *maika'i*-excellent. If this is not possible the ceremony could be continued the next day or at the most opportune time. The longer a situation is allowed to continue before having a ceremony the longer the process may take. Make *ho'oponopono* a part of your family life.
5. Food and music are appropriate to follow any *ho'oponopono* ceremony.
   A. ***Kalo***-taro root or ***poi***-cooked taro paste is symbolic of the family. Eating the *kino lau* of family enhances the realization of the value of a family and is the final ritual to **ho'omanamana**-to empower the success of *ho'oponopono*.

Pō-The After Life

When one has lived an honorable life and leaves the earthly realm, one's spirit travels to the western most point of an island called a ***leina***-spirit leap and is met there by one's ***'aumakua***-spirit ancestor. It is here that they leap together into *pō,* into the spirit realm of one's beloved family.

There Is No Hell

There is no concept of fire and brimstone in Hawaiian belief, only the thought of one's spirit being lonely and unloved. The mere act of loving an ancestor sets him free to enter *pō*, the spirit realm of the family. It therefore behooves us to nurture the best in our family, to love and to *hoʻoponopono*-set things right in this life time rather than be hurt and lonely in the next.

NOTES

CHAPTER THREE

ALOHA-LOVE

No other word in the Hawaiian Language has been so thoroughly interpreted and used so freely as the word *aloha*.

Aloha can be found in any standard English and Hawaiian dictionary and is generally interpreted to mean, *love*. As simple as it may seem, the definition of *love* in English is elusive. Ask anyone the meaning of love, and you'll get as many interpretations of love as you will of *aloha*. The simplicity of the meaning is not in the definition of the word, but in living it. By demonstrating the Hawaiian way to love, we can understand the Hawaiian way of aloha.

The Living Expression of Aloha

My first memory of aloha came as a young boy observing the manner in which my elders would express themselves when meeting. Seeing one another in the distance, they would call out affectionately in long breaths to one another, "Ui, eia nei!" And the host would call out, "Aloha mai!" "Come, come, come!" Gradually building to an emotional pitch, with eyes moistened with joy and fixed on one another, they would embrace, touching nose to cheek, expressing their feelings of aloha. This embrace and touching of face to face were repeated when leaving as well. Experiencing this would make sense of the components of the word aloha: "*Alo*" meaning face and "*hā*" meaning to breathe. To breathe upon the face. How better would one show so intimately that he or she cared?

The Dualism of Love
The dualism of love between husband and wife refers to the emotional or romantic and sexual expressions of love. Hawaiian historian Mary Kawena Pūkuʻi was once asked to speak on "the deep love of man and woman" and its relationship to sexual love. Kawena replied, "You mean it is time to put together what belongs together."

The celebration of life is the Hawaiian way of life. To pursue in all things a level of excellence is the mark of one beloved. The living of aloha by caring and touching is paralleled by romance and making love to its highest level. This is the Hawaiian ideal. The dualism of love is one in aloha. These ideas are poetically expressed in the **manaʻo**-meaning of our songs and chants. One's beauty is likened to a rare flower in the highest place, sought after by so many birds. Passion expressed as "moving waters of desire."

The Purpose of Aloha
The joys and pleasures of love as aloha have a true purpose in Hawaiian life. This celebration of love at its highest level of excellence blossoms in the foundation of a family, the cornerstone of Hawaiian culture.

There is an expression that goes, "He lei poina ʻole ke keiki." "A lei (garland) never forgotten is the beloved child." All children are loved as blossoms, **na pua**-flowers, of Hawaiʻi.

Even in the case of a childless union, the free exchange of charity by a family blessed with many children is practiced by the literal giving of one's own to another. All children are loved as blossoms of the union of romantic and sexual love, of *aloha*. What greater love is there than literally to give the blossoms of one's love to another?

Everlasting Love
The nurturing of love as aloha between husband and wife is perpetuated in the blossoms of their union, their children, who in turn carry on the ideals of *aloha* as demonstrated by their ancestors and practiced in their own lives. Love is everlasting. "E lei kau, e lei hoʻoilo i ke aloha." "Love is worn like a wreath through the summers and the winters."

Aloha ʻOe-May You Be Loved
The living expression aloha is love. Romantic and sexual love are one and of the highest ideal. Pursuing love as *aloha* at its highest level is a celebration of life, and from its union come the blossoms of everlasting love, a family, a new generation of *aloha*.

Touching and caring as a friend, lover and family member is the natural and Hawaiian way to love. ***Aloha ʻoe*-may you be loved!**

Sources:
  Nānā I Ke Kumu Vol. II
  ʻOlelo Noʻeau

NOTES

CHAPTER FOUR

PA‘AHANA-INDUSTRY

The Family
The value of work in a family establishes the foundation for *lōkāhi*-unity. Appreciation and excellence are also developed by the work ethic. Money should never be a reward on its own. Love, a sense of accomplishment, and appreciation for one's work should always be foremost. We all play a part and contribute to the whole.

Mana-Power and Work Ethics
The work ethic is a practical necessity for any person, family or society to succeed and excel in life. The work ethic of Hawai‘i is one of personal excellence. The power that comes from one's personal excellence is ***mana***. The successful increase of one's *mana* also reflects upon the quality of one's family and culture. The success of doing something well is always returned as increased *mana*.

Hawaiian and Western Work Ethics
As mentioned in the last paragraph, the Hawaiian work ethic is founded on personal excellence to increase one's *mana*. The increase of one's *mana* can only be accomplished subjectively. When an employee of a company develops a level of excellence at his craft and is rewarded with the power of sincere personal admiration, by his/her employer and/or fellow employees, he/she has successfully acquired *mana*. In contrast, the Western work ethic equates one's excellence with the increase of money or personal wealth. Money does not increase one's *mana*.

Apply the Hawaiian Work Ethic

The reality of today's Western-style objective economy in Hawai'i reflects a marked difference with the Hawaiian work ethic just described. Hawai'i works for *mana,* the West works for money. So how can we empower the present Western system with the Hawaiian ethic?

As stated in Chapter One we must be able to recognize the subjective and objective things in our lives. Remember that money, as well as the business of acquiring it, is impersonal and objective. Do not give it any meaning other than what it is. Since money is impersonal, you can work for or acquire as much or as little of it as you wish. Don't be embarrassed by the amount of money you want or have. Following is an example of how dealing with money on a personal level can work against you: You make hand carved koa sculptures and sell them for $100. Then a customer comes along with the most flattering compliments about your work and you think to yourself, "Since she's so nice, I'll sell my work for $50." What you have just purchased is $50 worth of appreciation from your customer. Remember the Western system of capitalism is impersonal and your intent is to sell your work, not *buy* appreciation. You can succeed in commerce if you strictly produce quality products and services. The recognition of your quality creates *mana,* while the increase of your bank account allows you to produce more business.

The Work Place

How do you succeed as an employee in a Western style company? Again, recognize the fact that your employer is in business for money and the interest of the stockholders. Don't expect to be loved as a daughter or a son. You must always strive to receive the highest amount of money and/or benefits for your quality of work.

Management

If you are limited in your development, upgrade your skills so that you can advance into management. In spite of your boss's Western-style business ethic, you can improve the output of your team by applying your subjective work ethic and elevate your position with your company. Should this approach be received unfavorably by your employer, then consider starting your own company or buying him/her out.

Your Own Company

Should you manage or own your company, you can personally empower the Hawaiian work ethic to work for you and your employees. It may seem that the West is blind to a Hawaiian style or subjective work ethic, but on the contrary there are model businesses that are applying similar techniques successfully. Simply put, the Hawaiian or subjective approach to business requires a personal commitment of an employer to his employees. Security, appreciation, a positive working environment, personal excellence, and compassion are all part of that commitment. Just as parents would care for their children, so too should the company care for its family of employees. The quality of a child reflects the quality of the parent. This personal approach would guarantee the commitment of excellence by one's employees and the marked advantage of financial success for the company.

CHAPTER FIVE

MAIKA'I - EXCELLENCE

The sound for excellence or what is supreme is *'i* (pronounced as "e" as in easy). The word *mai* means "to come" and *ka* means the article "the." *Maika'i* is an expression that beckons or confirms the presence of that which is supreme or excellent.

Male Symbol of Excellence

As a note of interest, a traditional symbol of *maika'i* between one man and another is the upright thumb and extension of the lower little finger. A man's excellence was equated with his male potency and therefore symbolized that potency by the image of an upright *ule*-penis. It is said that the popular Western thumbs up sign for all OK was derived from this Hawaiian symbol. Since the Vietnam era, the *shaka* sign has replaced the *maika'i* sign in popularity. This new adaptation of excellence, used by either sex, looks similar to the male *maika'i* symbol, but turned sideways. It was created originally to represent an island style victory or peace sign of the Vietnam War Era.

Personal Mana-Power

Personal excellence creates personal *mana*-power. Living to celebrate life is a natural way of excellence. Personal excellence applies to one's health, dress, or talents; in *aloha* as love and in making love; as a friend, husband, wife, father, mother, child or grandparent, *'aumakua* and *akua;* as well as in education, business and government.

Increase Your Excellence

Be thoughtful and kind when meeting elders, create time to listen to their hearts and minds, for in them is the wisdom of time. Express your aloha by touching nose to cheek, man to man, brother to brother, sister to brother, child to adult, woman to man, and woman to woman. Express your *aloha* to all who enter your home.

Always introduce your companion, whether family, friend or acquaintance, to those you meet. Always be appreciative and speak only words of goodwill and hope. Avoid too much chattering and those who are **waha nui**-loud. Use your ears, eyes, and senses to communicate with one another.

Pule-Prayer

Always address your parents and beloved of your ancestors in prayer. They have given you life and the wisdom of an ancient people. Use your prayer as an affirmation to celebrate life. Say it in Hawaiian or English with *aloha,* and close your prayer by saying, *'āmama*-it is finished, **ua noa**-it is free!

SUGGESTED READING

Atlas of Hawaii, Second Edition, University of Hawaii Press, Honolulu.

The Kumulipo, A Hawaiian Creation Chant, Beckwith, Martha Warren, University of Hawaii Press, Honolulu, 1981.

Stars Over Hawaii, Bryan, E. H. Jr., The Petroglyph Press, Hilo, Hawaii, 1977.

Chanting The Universe, Charlot, John, Hawaiian Religious Culture, Emphasis International Publisher, Hong Kong, 1983.

Na Pule Kahiko, Ancient Hawaiian Prayers, Gutmanis, June, Editions Limited Publisher, Honolulu, 1983.

Nā Inoa Hōkū, A Catalogue of Hawaiian and Pacific Star Names, Johnson, Rubellite Kawena, John Kaipo Mahelona, Topgallant Publishing Co., Ltd., Honolulu, 1975.

The Hawaiian Name Book, Ka'ano'i, Patrick, Robert Lokomaika'iokalani Snakenberg, Bess Press, Honolulu, 1988.

Hawaiian Antiquities, Malo, David, Bishop Museum Press, Honolulu, 1980.

'Ōlelo No'eau, Hawaiian Proverbs & Poetical Sayings, Pūku'i, Mary Kawena, Bishop Museum Press, Honolulu, 1983.

Hawaiian Dictionary, Pūku'i, Mary Kawena, Samuel H. Elbert, University of Hawaii Press, Honolulu, 1981.

Sites of O'ahu, Sterling, Elspeth P., Catherine C. Summers, Department of Anthropology, Department of Education, Bernice P. Bishop Museum, Honolulu, 1978.

Kingship and Sacrifice, Ritual and Society in Ancient Hawaii, Valeri, Valerio, Translated by Paula Wissing, The University of Chicago Press, Chicago and London, 1985.

Nānā I Ke Kumu (Look To The Source) Volume I & II, Pūku'i, Mary Kawena, E. W. Haertig, M.D., Catherine A. Lee, Hui Hanai Publishing, Honolulu.

Kū Kanaka, Stand Tall, A Search for Hawaiian Values, Kanahele, George Hu'eu Sanford, University of Hawai'i Press and Waiaha Foundation.

NOTES

NOTES

NOTES

NOTES

NOTES

NOTES

NOTES

NOTES

NOTES